Sheep Theory:

Think Outside

The Flocks

Exercises to promote innovative thinking

Greg Frisbee

ISBN: 979-8-218-02663-9 (paperback)

For my son Max.

"When I was young, my ambition was to be one of the people who made a difference in this world. My hope is to leave the world a little better for having been there."

-Jim Henson

PROLOGUE

"Shoot for the moon, and even if you miss, you will land amongst the stars."

MY GRANDMOTHER USED TO say that to me. She was always my biggest supporter, encouraging me to take risks and go for my dreams, or at least to try.

With this book, I'm hoping to provide that kind of support for you. I want to give you ideas and inspiration that will help you break through the blocks you may be facing, whether these are creative blocks or blocks that have nothing to do with your creativity.

I'm confident that there are always creative solutions to almost any problem and creative exercises that can help us find them. In this book, I will share my favorite ways to spark my mind to work and create differently, and to overcome the obstacles that get in my way.

Thank you for joining me on this adventure!

WHO AM I?

"Your performer (author) today has been making a lot of noise around the Orlando area... the neighbors have complained. He has made headlines in Europe... although he denies the allegations and has been seen by Fortune 500 companies... ordering a burger and fries. Here he is, the one, the only, the legend... in his own mind - GREG FRISBEE!"

Some version of this is how announcers and emcees have introduced me around the globe. My name is Greg Frisbee and I am a comedy juggler, cool fire eater, and innovative magician. For the last 25 years, I have made my living as a professional idiot... errr, creative silly person. I have had the privilege of performing in more than 40 countries, all 50 states, and on cruises around the world.

My entire career and, as it turns out, most of my life, has been filled with creativity, looking at the world in different ways, and developing creative solutions to problems I faced. I've used my creative techniques to perform and create unique, sometimes dangerous or absurd stunts, such as fire hands, where I light my hands on fire and juggle knives, or safely launching rubber chickens 100 feet in the air and catching them in a fried chicken bucket helmet. This creative approach has allowed me to travel the globe doing ridiculously awesome shows in some pretty incredible places, such as Dubai, South Korea and Ireland.

So how did a super shy kid with no creative ambitions end up here?

I often feel like my career path chose me rather than me choosing to be a performer. When I was a kid, I was picked on a lot, and I had to find creative solutions to work through those challenges. Humor and showmanship turned out to be my most successful strategies.

As a teen, I learned magic. I enjoyed the creative process of putting together tricks and figuring out illusions. When I graduated from high school, I saw my first variety performers and was drawn to try. I had no idea what I was doing at first, but I knew early on that this was the path for me.

In pushing myself to step outside of my comfort zone, I created a new and larger comfort zone in which to live and I started to learn all I could about being creative.

As I headed into a creative career, I faced plenty of opposition. Throughout my early career, I experienced challenges and adversity, mostly from people saying "you can't do that," or something along those lines of resistance.

But what other people said didn't matter to me. I knew in me that I could do it and I wouldn't take "no" for an answer. With perseverance and by being stubborn and determined, I set out to follow and cultivate my creativity in various forms. It has kept me going for nearly 30 years.

The creative process for me may be different than it is for you, as we each have our own way that works best for us. We need to learn to develop that individual mindset and think outside the flocks.

No, not outside the box, although that's good, too. But outside the flocks — outside the habitual patterns and expectations created by our communities and environment.

And not simply outside one flock, but outside the many that make up our life and our normal day-to-day patterns. We have lots of flocks: the flock of family, the flock of friends, the flock of co-workers, the flock of teachers and so on. When you're overcoming creative obstacles, you need to look at a variety of methods to find solutions, but you also need to think outside the flocks.

To get myself into a creative state of mind, I try to clear whatever workspace I am going to be working in. I typically do not like a lot of outside noise or distractions, though I can occasionally listen to music, but it depends on the project I am working on. If I am scripting or anything where I am collecting thoughts, I need silence. If I am building a prop or practicing a trick, I like to have music.

Making the leap from an idea in my head to some sort of physical action usually takes some time. When I have an initial idea, it usually sits and lingers a bit and if I find that I am thinking about it a lot or the idea keeps coming up into conversations, then I give it a bit more developmental thought.

I may experiment with building if it is a prop, create different versions of an idea, or write out those ideas and sketches into my journals and do some associations through mind mapping. The ideas may stay as a thought in my head for a day, weeks, months or even longer before I take it further.

When I am beginning to create something, I do not always have a finished product or end goal in mind. I *do*, however, have an idea of what I want to do or create. I may want to create a puppet, build a prop or new show structure, but not necessarily have a finished puppet show or even a full use for the prop I am building or know where I'll put it in a show.

Sometimes I create the idea for the sake of creating and will figure out where it fits, if it fits, later.

When I experience creative blocks, I find that one of the best solutions for me is to step away from a project for a bit and then come back to it. Sometimes the timing isn't right or I am not looking at it in the right way and giving it a bit of space allows me to see it more clearly.

When asked if I had to do it all over again, I would not change the path I have taken or even the challenges and hardships I have faced and had to overcome. With the journey I am on, I have been given opportunities that many don't get to have, and the rewards have been great. Not the least of these rewards has been that I have learned to see and appreciate the uniqueness and creativity in life all around me.

ABOUT THIS BOOK

On the pages that follow are more than 50 techniques that will lead you to more and better creative thinking. I hope that these tools will give you innovative ways to tackle your challenges. I want to help you find your solutions and break through the blocks you may be having in your problem-solving process, personally or within your business.

Some of these are techniques I have created. Some of them were taught to me and some I learned over my 20-plus years as an international entertainer.

These tools have helped me, and some of them have helped others. I know that some of them will now help YOU.

Perhaps you already know some of these techniques, but they have been tucked away and need to be dusted off. This book is intended to be a tool to help you spark not only new ideas, but maybe also refresh your memory on something you already knew but have forgotten.

A lot of these ideas are simple, but simple doesn't always mean easy. Sometimes you need to revisit a method you have tried, even if it felt like it failed or wasn't for you. Solutions take work, dedication, determination, and sometimes just a bit more time. I encourage you to give these ideas a try. If they don't work the first time, try them again.

Interspersed within the lessons, I've also included thoughts from other creative people from various fields. I asked them a series of questions about creativity and overcoming hurdles and these are their responses. Their insights will offer you some different perspectives. You can find the complete list of question, as well as more information on the respondents, in the appendix.

As you reach each question and read the answers, I encourage you to think about the question and come up with your own answers. Write down the questions and answers and keep them in your journal. This narrative will be eye opening for you, helping you understand why you do what you do and letting you see how you already are using tools to overcome creative blocks.

1. KEEP AN IDEA JOURNAL

HAVE A WAY TO record and write your ideas down. An idea journal lets you collect and write down ideas whenever they strike. It can be a physical journal or an app on your phone, like a voice memo or note taker. It must be something that you have easy access to most, if not ALL of the time.

I find that I use the Notes app on my phone as my current go-to journal. I used to keep a blank book art journal with me or a notebook relatively handy, but my phone is almost always in my pocket, in my backpack or in my hand, I will then eventually transfer the notes from my phone to my notebooks.

If you scribble ideas on lots of papers in various places, put them into a folder or binder. Ideally, I encourage you to have a journal that you write in regularly and record all of your ideas. You need a place for spontaneous or structured thoughts that you write out, and in which to create your doodles and mind maps.

It also helps to add a date to your entries. This will make it easier to look back on entries from a particular time period. Ideas can and absolutely WILL strike at any time, and usually when you are not thinking about anything in particular.

You may see something that sparks an idea you were working on, a brand new idea you want to work on later or something you just want to remember.

2. Save All Your Ideas

THIS IS A SIMPLE extension of the previous technique: save *all* your ideas.

The benefit of having journals for your ideas is that items you write or create now, which may feel irrelevant or unimportant, can spark inspiration later for another project.

I've found myself looking through old journals countless times, seeing ideas that I keep coming back to as recurring themes. Even stranger are times when I stumble across an idea that I don't even remember writing about, only to find that I actually implemented it in my life or my show subconsciously. Journals are interesting glimpses into our brain's thinking process.

Go over your journal and list of ideas every day for a predetermined length of time. As an example, set aside 10 minutes a day to review your thoughts. Alternatively, you may establish a daily goal of developing one of your ideas.

Having a list of ideas on hand will allow you to write down thoughts whenever you need to. Write temporary notes on your phone or pieces of paper and then add them to your list when you return home to keep track of everything. To some people, having a list of ideas on their phone is a convenient way to remember them. A tiny notebook can also be carried in your pocket.

Don't let an inspiration pass you by without acting on it. Don't judge or over-analyze ideas that come your way. Just write them down, then let them rest for a while. You never know when you're going to need that new idea.

3. Keep a Dream Journal

DREAMS CAN BE A tremendous source of inspiration and new ideas and may be a huge help to overcome your blocks if you pay attention to them. Most of our dreams are quickly forgotten the next day but if you start to regularly write down your dreams as soon as you wake up, you'll find it increases your dream recall.

When you get up in the morning, grab a notebook and start writing. You don't need to write the dream out fully, because that gets confusing and you'll usually forget the details. Instead, just record any specific images, words or thoughts as they come to mind.

If your memories of the dream start slipping away, let them go. They might reappear or another dream recollection could surface. Dreams are a great source of knowledge about what our brain is processing. You may dream about the end of your project or some outlandish idea that you could refine into a reality.

The more you keep track of your dreams, the more vivid and in-depth your memories and recall will become. Dreams have been a source of inspiration for many artists throughout history, and they could inspire YOU!

"Creativity is thinking up new things.

Innovation is doing new things."

-Theodore Levitt

4. Look at What Others Are Doing

WHEN I WAS FIRST performing and had no idea how to structure comedy or create a show, I tried to watch as many performers as I could. I also watched old vaudeville movies. I watched Charlie Chaplin, Buster Keaton and Harold Lloyd films and studied their structure for clowning and creating. I read books about them and tried to learn who they were and broke down what I found funny about them. My grandmother mentioned to me in later years that I reminded her of Harold Lloyd.

Sometimes you don't need to reinvent the wheel or start from scratch. Sometimes others have created a starting point and can give you a head start on your project.

Don't steal other people's ideas. However, if you are trying to create a new kind of lightbulb, you don't need to figure out how a lightbulb works, because we already have that information to start from.

Looking into the lives of other creatives might help you better understand your own process. I bet you will discover some interesting similarities. In addition, you may discover new ways of looking at the world or expressing yourself.

Pick an artist you admire and study *their* creative process. Try to learn from them by reading books, watching them or listening to interviews with them. Select someone who is completely out of your sphere of expertise. This can help you on the path to think outside the flocks.

A writer may designate a specific time of day to write when their inspiration strikes. A thought leader may take a long walk after lunch to clear their heads and do their best creative thinking.

Q & A With Creatives

———ele———

Q: WHAT DO YOU think it means to be creative?

Alan, Innovator & Entrepreneur: To be creative, one has to simply unleash their imagination. The creative process starts in the mind and is expressed in infinite ways.

———————

Nick, Producer & Creative Director: Being creative is allowing your mind to wander freely and imagine something that is either not already there or better than what is existing.

———————

Rob, Program Director & Morning Radio Show Host: I think to be creative is to be open to possibilities. In my job, it's necessary to be flexible and be ready to cover breaking news. It's important to think about how to convey that information as quickly and reliably as possible while also doing so in a manner that maintains listenership.

———————

Barry, Chief Architect/Co-Founder: I tend to think in literal terms. To be creative means to have the ability to create — to make something using what is available to you, whether that is building something physically out of tangible materials, or mentally thinking and coming up with a solution to a problem, or an issue at hand. It can be imaginative or practical. It can be a lot of work.

———————

Katrin, CEO: Creativity is therapy. Therapy everyone should have access to beyond the age of a child. Creativity is the gateway to your dreams, your imagination, and sometimes your desires you don't dare to dream of. If we allow ourselves to be creative, we can create a world of possibilities. And not only for one moment, but sometimes for a lifetime.

———————

Boswick, Circus Performer & Clown: I think creativity is letting your mind wander to solve a problem. It's simply an obstacle. I think creativity is put on a pedestal but everyone has it and uses it. A school teacher becomes creative in teaching kids to get excited about science. A construction worker finds a different way to hang a door they never thought of or have seen. Creativity is trusting, listening and encouraging your wandering mind.

———————

Elisa, Speaker, Author & Designer: Creativity expresses aspects of the human experience through a creator's chosen medium. Creativity calls forth a prophetic vision of the past, present, or future that brings us into deeper and wider experiences of what it means to be human.

5. Have Separate Rooms

———— *ℓℓℓ* ————

CREATE SEPARATE SPACES IN your work life for creating and critiquing. Have one location where you do the initial work and a second location for refining.

I'm not talking about working from separate rooms with a work partner or creative team, though sometimes that can be helpful when you all come together to discuss and critique what you have created at a later time.

Having a place to think and create without critiquing, editing, judgment or any utterance of the word "NO" is awesome.

The idea is that you create, write, brainstorm or work on your project in a space where there is no initial editing allowed. No rewriting, no crossing out ideas, no erasing or doubling back... just create.

Realize that it is okay to create and allow yourself to make mistakes. When you pause and edit in the moment, you are disrupting the flow. Remember, a bad idea may lead to a good idea if you allow the full train of thought.

If you only have one place in which to work, give yourself a time frame in order to switch between creating and revising. But ideally, having separate rooms — one for creating, brainstorming and coming up with ideas and another for critiquing — allows you to wear different processing hats.

The separate rooms can be two rooms at your house, a room at home and a cafe down the street, or even the difference between being indoors and outdoors.

Once you are done with the creative time, step into the other room or other mindset, and then and only then look at what you've done with a more critical editing eye to make revisions.

6. Generate Lots of Ideas

Generate lots of ideas, and cut your bad ones later.

People tend to quit searching for a solution once they've found one that works. They don't think about their problem anymore because it's been resolved. But sometimes going the extra mile and looking for alternatives leads to greater results, or just multiple good results that you can plug and play.

It's never too late to look at your current situation and see what else could be done.

When I am trying to figure out a solution to a challenge I am facing, I create as much as I can, metaphorically throwing a bunch of stuff against the wall to see what sticks.

In the midst of the Covid-19 crisis when my work disappeared overnight, I quickly pivoted to, "Ok, what's next?" Sometimes, creative problem-solving is a numbers game. The more ideas you have, the better.

Comedian and TV show host, Seth Meyers, does a monologue five days a week, averaging 15-20 jokes per monologue. He has a staff of writers who create hundreds of jokes, plus whatever he writes to make up those 20 jokes. The writers know that each day they have a low percentage of having all or even any of their jokes making the cut, but eventually they hit a home run.

Think quantity over quality. Write out or talk out or use some other way to record your thoughts, and try to come up with as many ideas around your topic as you can.

First, try using a time limit, say, 15 minutes. Through trial and error, you will find the magic number that works for you. It might be 5 minutes or an hour or more that you need to get all of your thoughts out on a particular topic.

When working on quantity over quality, it is important to put yourself in your creating space/room, not your critique room (see #5).

Still, don't obsess over finding alternatives to the point that you're never satisfied with any of them!

7. Find the Missing Link

I AM NOT TALKING about THAT missing link or Bigfoot, but sometimes the solution to your creative challenge is just as elusive. Make sure that the roadblock you are hitting with your creative endeavors is not a something or someone that you are missing. Take a look at the problem and your end goal and evaluate whether you have all the pieces of the puzzle.

- Are you missing information?
- Is there a tool or technique that you could use that would make your goal easier to achieve?
- Is there a person with a skill set who could help accomplish the project or idea?

Take a look at your goals and see what is missing. What would it take to implement that missing piece? Is it is a tool or a person issue? Do you need an investment, other than time, to reach a different solution for your overall idea?

Q & A With Creatives

———ele———

Q: Do you have any tricks or tips for keeping yourself interested and excited about your projects or work?

Alan, Innovator & Entrepreneur: Every few years I visit a trade show that is completely outside of my industry. It sparks new ideas, puts me in a completely different environment and I get to meet some very interesting people. Large trade shows typically attract companies that are serious players in their industry. It's fun to learn new things for the sake of learning and be curious about what others do for a living and why.

— — — — —

Nick, Producer & Creative Director: I think about my end user (the audience) and the responses I hope to create in them. Whether it be joy or nostalgia or self-reflection, knowing that there is a reason for me to create that is outside of myself gives me all the motivation I need.

— — — — —

Rob, Program Director & Morning Radio Show Host: If ever I feel I am in need of a creative recharge, I sample the work of my peers. I go online and stream a similar program in another city or state. I think it is important to see and hear what others in your field are doing to see what you might need to work on or improve in yourself. In addition, it is also a good idea to talk or have meetings with others in your field. This can also be very helpful to vent and to give yourself a pep charge.

Barry, Chief Architect/Co-Founder: I love my work, and always find it fascinating. I like problem solving and innovating. However, I did hit many walls when things weren't going in the direction I hoped for, or development wasn't coming along fast enough. I would do more research to stay interested. Is there a different technology to apply? A new logic?

More often than not, this research was tangential to the actual work I needed to do. But, it was a beneficial distraction. It took my head out of the problem I was in and allowed me to re-think and refresh.

Elisa, Speaker, Author & Designer: Practice radical self-care. When we are stressed, our brains solve problems using the path of least resistance which means thinking and doing as we already know. Creativity requires a playful spirit that only comes when we feel rested.

Boswick, Circus Performer & Clown: Just start. The smallest movement toward a project pays off immensely. If you want to write a book, write down 10 titles. If you want to be an actor, sign up for an acting class. Just make a start.

I'm a fan of classes. Writers have writing groups, I am pretty sure the biggest benefit is that you have to present your work week after week. In acting classes, you have to prepare a scene week after week. In an exercise class, you do what the instructor says.

Q: How do you stay focused?

Katrin, CEO: Engaging my audience. Listening to their needs.

I now love going live on Facebook, checking in and asking questions. It is imperative to keep in touch with your audience to make a business fly. I like the friends I made along the way. Building healthy and lasting relationships is important. I also figured out to just be me and no one else. Super helpful and what a time saver. :-)

8. Collaborate

COLLABORATING WITH OTHERS CAN help in the creative process. The saying goes, "Two heads are better than one," but how about adding three or four?

Of course, there's a limit — you don't want too many people on a project and how many is right will depend on the project.

For example, I would limit a writing group for comedy to four people. I would give us two hours for our collaboration meeting. Each person can be the focus of the group for thirty minutes, writing for one another.

Or if everyone is working on one person's routine or a specific topic for the time, give each person the floor and focus for thirty minutes. It can help to treat the session like the create and critique rooms. Allow your full thoughts to come out, judgement free. Then find the time to critique after.

Make sure that whoever is the focus of the collaborative group has final say if there is not a consensus. Talking to others is a great method to generate new ideas.

Another idea is to create an accountability group that follows a similar process. You can meet up physically or virtually, once a week or once a month or whatever works.

Ideas and inspiration can also come through socializing with friends or coworkers. You may have a buddy who is particularly adept at bouncing ideas around.

Recently I was working on a puppetry video project as a way to build content and work on a new creative outlet. A friend approached me, liked the idea and asked if he could join me. I used my YES to invite him on board with my project and collaborate. That yes led to a video production company wanting to get involved. Before I knew it, he had pitched us to a client of his. Suddenly, I was part of a commercial venture for a media company overseas. All through saying yes and exploring collaboration.

Talking to a complete stranger can also help you see things from a different angle. New ideas can be gained via conversing with someone who comes from a different background.

Think about who you want to collaborate with before you start. Is there a specific person with whom you've had a positive experience brainstorming with?

Also, I recommend staying away from folks that drain your energy and aren't really willing to commit or open to try new ideas. Try to make acquaintances with people who share your interests.

This is a good workout for you and your team, all of whom will benefit from it. Hopefully you'll all go away with new ideas and sparks of creativity.

9. Learn to Juggle

When I was around 12, a friend of mine juggled three pool balls. I thought it was the coolest thing and wanted to learn how to do it. But I could not get it no matter how hard I tried and so I gave up on it, thinking it was something I just couldn't do.

Years later, I was performing close up magic as a street performer in Boston and saw jugglers again on a regular basis. I vowed that I would finally learn how to do it. I stood over my couch one day with 3 tennis balls and kept trying and trying until I could get a basic three ball juggle.

With that small victory, my mind was unlocked. I wanted to try more and more tricks and then eventually move on to other juggling props like clubs and spinning balls. I became obsessed with learning it all. I could see the rewards every time I succeeded at learning a new trick. Eventually, juggling became one of the core skills of my career, with over twenty years of performances that include juggling.

Learning to juggle was a challenge for me, but it opened doors that changed my life. More importantly, it changed my way of thinking. I am not telling you to learn to juggle because it will give you a career as a juggler, but focusing on juggling will help clear your mind of blocks you may be facing, so pick up a few juggling balls or rolled up socks and LEARN TO JUGGLE.

Juggling is a great way to get your mind and creativity flowing. I don't mean you need to be juggling crazy patterns or building a routine with rubber chickens. Juggling has many, many benefits for the creative process.

It has the ability to relax you (once you are juggling, not when you are dropping all the time while trying to learn.)

Juggling has all of these added benefits: it can decompress you; it can change your mindset; it can improve your rhythm; it can improve your balance; it can sharpen your focus and your concentration; it's compact exercise.

In addition, juggling literally makes you smarter. Juggling is one of the few physical exercises that can cause your brain to actually grow!

HOW TO JUGGLE 3 BALLS

| Start with two balls in the right hand and one ball in the left. | Toss ball #1 from the right hand to the left. | As ball #1 is landing, toss ball #2 into the air. | Toss ball #2 from the left hand to the right. |
| As ball #2 is landing in the right hand, toss ball #3 into the air. | Toss ball #3 from the right hand to the left hand. As it lands, toss ball #1 into air. | Toss ball #1 from the left hand to the right hand. | Continue the cycle until you can do it smoothly. |

STEP 1: ONE BALL

Toss one ball back and forth between your hands. Practicing with one ball is a good way to get comfortable and perfect the tossing back-and-forth motion you will need to juggle three balls.

Work on tossing the ball so that it goes up at an angle, peaks just above your head and then travels down at an angle into your opposite hand. When the ball lands in your hand, scoop your hand up into the air to toss the ball back to the other hand.

STEP 2: TWO BALLS

Once you've got the tossing motion down with one ball, it is time to try adding in a second ball.

Hold a ball in each hand. Then, using your dominant hand to start, toss one of the balls up at an angle, so that it peaks just above your head.

When the first ball peaks, toss the second ball up, using the same motion as your first throw. Catch the first ball you threw, and then the second, so that both balls end up in the opposite hand from the one they started in.

STEP 3: THREE BALLS

Don't move on to three balls until you feel comfortable and are consistently throwing the two balls in the air with the crossing pattern as described in Step 2.

Hold two balls in your dominant hand (the one you write with or naturally grab an item with) and the third in your other hand.

Toss one of the paired up balls into the air (as you did when practicing with one ball and again when practicing with two) You want to toss it so that it goes just above eye level to the other hand.

Throw the ball in your opposite hand into the air after the first ball peaks (as you did when practicing with two).

Right after you toss the first ball, toss the ball in your opposite hand into the air. Try to toss it with the same amount of force as you used to toss the first ball. Toss it at an angle so that its trajectory ends in your other hand.

Toss the third and last ball from your dominant hand into the air as the second ball is coming down to your first hand.

Toss it in the same way as you tossed the first two balls and do it immediately after the second ball peaks.

Catch the balls in the order that you threw them. Each ball should end up in the opposite hand from where it started. If your left hand had two juggling balls in it when you started, those two balls should be in your right hand now.

Congratulations, this is a juggle!

You can continue the pattern by throwing the next ball in the sequence, as the third ball is peaking, throw the next ball and onward you go.

Helpful Juggling Tips

- Pretend you're scooping ice cream for the hand motion of throwing the ball back and forth.
- Practice above a table, couch or if you are at home, a bed so that you aren't always having to bend down to pick up the dropped balls. You will likely drop a LOT in the beginning.
- Don't practice near breakable items.
- Practice by counting out loud. Label each ball with 1, 2, 3 or A, B, C or have three different colored juggling balls and count those numbers, letters or colors when going through the pattern of juggling.
- Don't get discouraged if you can't juggle three balls right away. Learning to juggle, like lots of things, takes a bit of time and practice, and I am sure you will get there.

10. Doodle

HERE'S A FUN ONE: doodling. What is doodling, you ask? Doodling as defined by the Merriam-Webster Dictionary is: "an aimless or casual scribble, design, or sketch."

While you are sitting and brainstorming, thinking or staring at the wall wondering what to write in your journal or what to add to the project, scribble away.

It can be a pattern, swirly lines, a simple sketch or anything as long as it doesn't take too much focus. It is not something to put lots of drawing detail into; it's a way to let your mind wander.

People who doodle are often more productive and focused, so I say, doodle away. Doodling can help you find solutions to problems and also help you with remembering thoughts and ideas.

Just be sure that you don't turn in a report covered with your doodles to your teacher or boss.

"I have been doodling with ink and watercolor on paper all my life. It's my way of stirring up my imagination to see what I find hidden in my head.

I call the results dream pictures, fantasy sketches, and even brain-sharpening exercises."

-Maurice Sendak

11. Draw Circles

ell

SOMETIMES WE THINK WE have to get it perfect the first time out. Just like allowing first drafts, here is a fun exercise that continues the previous doodling idea.

Take a piece of paper and trace a circle of something relatively small, maybe the lid of a bottle cap or something a little bit larger. Trace that circle as many times as you can fit onto a page, ideally at least 20 or so.

Within each circle, draw a picture. There is no right or wrong to this, but it should be fast, so set a timer for about 1-2 minutes and see how many of the circles you can fill with a doodle or drawing.

Did it become harder to figure out what to do as you went along with each drawing?

Did you find yourself thinking of how to be more creative in each one?

"You can't use up creativity... The more you use, the more you have."

-Maya Angelou

12. Ask A Kid

IF YOU ARE FINDING it hard to think like a kid, try talking to one and ask them questions.

Children hold a unique perspective and have a certain creative and fresh way of looking at the world and seeing with their younger eyes.

Ask a kid how they might tackle a particular challenge you are facing.

Think about how you might simplify a problem down to more basic principles so that a kid could more easily understand it.

I do not personally believe, as others do, that children are more creative before society takes that away. I *do* think that children see things and speak with an honest, often unfiltered, perspective, filled with innocence of understanding that can open up the door to new ways of thinking.

As we grow up, that is often put aside for our other responsibilities.

Don't run out and build a spaceship made out of cardboard however, just because some kid told you to.

The idea of this exercise isn't to do what the child says. It's to get your own thinking process onto a more unfiltered and unconventional path.

13. THINK LIKE A KID

———— *ee* ————

Do you remember your childhood? How far back can you remember?

Take a few moments and close your eyes and think of how you used to play and the toys you would play with. Think about the games you would play and the stories you and your friends invented.

I remember going outside to play with my toy cars, racing them thru the sand dunes. I remember my toy ray gun that I imagined was given to me to fend off the impending alien invasion and playing with my friends to create our own worlds and magical villages.

Think back to your childhood memories. Those times were probably, mostly, hopefully carefree and fun, with no major cares in the world. We need to release our obstacles and burdens to unlock that gift of childhood innocence again. Remember to let your imagination go and also grow.

How often are we told, "Stop acting like a child?" Maybe it stopped in adolescence or maybe it lasted through your adult life, but when being creative or finding creative solutions, it's actually a good thing to sometimes act like a child. At one point, and maybe one you can define, you stopped acting like a child. To overcome creative blockages, maybe it is time to start acting like a child again and create those magical worlds.

- Let your mind wander.
- Say what you mean without fear of censor.
- Play.
- Seek out new experiences.
- Plan adventures.

The Marshmallow Challenge was invented by Peter Skillman and popularized by Tom Wujec in his TED Talk.

The Challenge is pretty simple. Teams are given: 10 pieces of dry spaghetti, one yard of masking tape, one yard of string and a single marshmallow. With 18 minutes on a timer, the goal is to build the tallest, freestanding structure and have a marshmallow at the top.

The exercise is used to show creativity and to promote collaboration and teamwork. When challenged against business graduate students, kindergartners consistently do better. The business graduates tend to over plan and seek to control the build and can often even run out of time with over planning.

Kids approach the problem with fresh ideas and have creative solutions. They will get right to building and work through trial and error. They collaborate more freely and often build more creative structures.

14. SAY YES, INSTEAD OF MAYBE

———*ell*———

TRY TO GET IN the habit of saying YES!

The word YES has a lot of power behind it, as does the word NO. (We will talk about the power of NO next.)

YES is magic. It will open doors and present opportunities to you. If you are afraid to say yes, you will miss those opportunities. This happens in life as well as in the creative process.

Saying YES has provided me with many creative opportunities, as well as the chance to travel internationally extensively. Once, saying YES! allowed me, on very short notice, to perform my ball-spinning routine on the stage of the prestigious Shanghai Grand Theatre in China. It's still a highlight of my career, and a memory that I might never have had without the willingness to say YES spontaneously.

We say NO all too often because of a fear of failure. When we say YES, we have the ability and power to create more, and more doors will open.

If you are too busy saying NO or MAYBE, to yourself or coworkers, you are stifling the creative process, shutting yourself down and potentially losing opportunities. When you shut down the creative input of others, you may do more harm than good, as they may be less likely to contribute more ideas.

When I was first starting out in performing and following my creative path, I said MAYBE too much. I also said, "I'm not ready," and "I'll do that someday." What I learned was that no one ever feels ready, and someday rarely comes.

One of my dreams when I first started performing at 19 was to study at the Ringling Brothers Clown College program in Florida. I thought this would kickstart my performing endeavors professionally, giving me the training I needed, and so much more. I would have been right!

I went so far as to get the brochure mailed to me, filled out the application and sent it off. I was accepted. Then I had that crippling feeling of 'I'm not ready," and "'I'll do it another time."

I didn't go to Clown College, and the program ended up shutting down the next year. I missed my opportunity, because I thought there would be another day when I felt ready.

We have to learn to take risks and say yes. Stepping outside our comfort zone expands our comfort zone.

I learned early in my 20s, when my father passed away at a young age, that tomorrow is not a promise or a guarantee. Saying YES to opportunities has become my go-to motto ever since.

15. EMBRACE THE POWER TO SAY NO

THERE IS ALSO POWER in the word NO! It is a powerful statement and one that can instantly shut down the creative process, but what if saying NO actually aids your creativity?

I don't mean to say no in terms of the development or the creative process itself or opportunities that may present themselves. I mean, say NO to distractions that deflect you from the task at hand.

How many times are you just starting to get somewhere when someone asks you for help or if you want to go out to lunch or hang out or whatever? We have to learn to say NO.

We have to get over our fear of appearing mean or unfriendly. We have to give our projects and our creative time precedence.

Saying NO is the only way to protect your time. Being afraid to say NO will prevent your success, almost as clearly as being afraid to say YES will.

"The worst enemy to creativity is self-doubt."

-Sylvia Plath

16. CHOOSE CREATIVITY

—eℓℓ—

CHOOSE CREATIVITY MAY SEEM like a weird statement, but it *is* a choice, just like saying, "Let's look at this logically." Making a choice to choose creativity may put you in the mindset to think more creatively. Switching your creativity on and off might take practice, but it can be done.

The way you become an expert and build your creativity arsenal is by doing, over and over and over again. Supposedly, becoming an expert takes 10,000 hours of practice. I was also told that you have to do 100 bad shows before you'll do a good one. When I was learning to play the piano, juggle or teach myself magic tricks, repetition was key. Learning involves trial and error. It's a process. Sometimes you try to be perfect in your idea and get it the way you want right out of the gate. Sometimes you just need to do a lot, and create in numbers.

Creativity is like a muscle. It works all day, every day and really doesn't take a break. But how strong that muscle becomes depends on how you are choosing to use it. Choose creativity and put in the time to make it a regular way of thinking.

Q & A With Creatives

_____eee_____

Q: As a creative person/having a job that requires creative solutions, what was one of the toughest obstacles you had to overcome?

Rob, Program Director & Morning Radio Show Host: One of the toughest things to overcome is that every day I must go on air and be upbeat and entertaining. Sometimes I might feel down, tired or grumpy, but it is important to never let that affect your ability to inform and entertain your listeners. It is my mission to wake people up and let them know what's going in their world.

Alan, Innovator & Entrepreneur: Simple. Talking in front of people. Always has been one of the biggest struggles in my life. Maybe following a career path that forced me to stand in front of people with a microphone wasn't a smart choice, but it looked fun!

Nick, Producer & Creative Director: Funding is always a challenge. So it public critique. If you are fortunate enough to be high enough profile, you will inevitably encounter individuals who do not like your work. As for money... well, there's never gonna be enough, so you might as well stop worrying about it and get on with it.

Elisa, Speaker, Author & Designer: Creating ideas is not the hard part, that just takes a commitment to intentional daydreaming. Communicating vision, however, is a whole other matter. Getting others to see what you see requires skill and can be a frustrating process.

Barry, Chief Architect/Co-Founder: The toughest obstacle was getting started. It is one thing to have an idea to do something in a better way. It is another thing entirely to actually come up with a way to do it in real life. You can't enchant computers with magic to make something happen.

My business partner and I would ideate for a very long time trying to nail down specifically how our application would do what we would hope it would do. Then it was a very long period of trial and error trying to find software and technology that could be applied to make it work. Finally, we found some tools that started to work as we had hoped, and we could move forward.

Boswick, Circus Performer & Clown: Being self-employed is the toughest part. I've been broke so many times and wondered why I can't just make a normal living like a normal person. I've had many side jobs over the years so that I could perform. I have persevered over many years and created an incredible life and incredible family.

Katrin, CEO: I would say time management (I'm a homeschooling Mama). Also, believing in myself. If you have difficulties believing in yourself, sometimes they can only be overcome by actually revealing those fears, saying "I'm afraid to go out and do this." It's a bit counterintuitive, but sometimes the only way to find the strength is by putting yourself out there and letting it grow with exposure.

17. Turn It Upside-Down

HAVE YOU EVER BEEN working on a puzzle and noticed that by looking at it from different angles or upside down, you immediately recognized where a piece belonged? It's time to apply the same logic to whatever project you're working on.

Turning something upside down to see how it looks from a different viewpoint may be a great approach to break through a creativity barrier

Re-imagining and changing perspective can help you identify patterns you missed from your existing viewpoint, whether you're turning things around physically or altering how you look at it in your head.

Our minds have a slew of pattern-making behaviors that frequently hide other, more subtle patterns at work. Changing the orientation of objects can obscure the more evident patterns and allow these additional patterns to emerge.

For example, you could wonder, "How would this problem look if the least important part was now the most important?" Would that change how I approached the problem?

Here are some examples and exercises:

- Look at a puzzle from various angles.
- Look at an abstract painting from all sides and see if it changes your view of how you interpret it.
- Play with a Rubik's cube and constantly look at all the different sides.

- Try to read upside down.

18. Follow A to B to C

OVERCOMING OBSTACLES CAN BE as simple as starting and having a proper order.

Start with step A and then step B is next. Or the next step will reveal itself. Don't jump to work on step B and exclude step A. Step C is not necessarily going to be obvious while you're still on step A, so allow yourself the process. Take the steps in the order that is needed. Work toward your end goal step-by-step.

For example, you can't learn to juggle without first getting some objects to juggle (scarves, balls, clubs). Once you have those items, you can work on the technique of tossing one and catching it. You can learn how to move your arms and how to throw from one hand to the other. You have to work on the throws, on breathing and on your focus. You can eventually work to throw two and figure out the pattern needed, and then move on to three or even more.

There are many steps to the process of leaning proper juggling techniques, and they need to be in a certain order for you to succeed. The same is true for many other projects.

19. READ A BOOK

—ele—

READ A BOOK. FIND someone who inspires you.

Learn from someone who worked on a similar idea as what you are trying to do.

Look for words and stories that spark your imagination.

You never know where inspiration might be found. You could be mid-sentence in a memoir or an adventure novel when the solution to your block pops into your head.

If you don't want to read or think you don't have time to read, listen to an audio book while you're driving or at the end of your day. If that seems still like too much, break it down into smaller chunks by listening to a podcast that will entertain or inspire or take you to different worlds.

Q & A With Creatives

Q: **HAVE YOU EVER felt like your own expectations stopped you from being creative?**

Nick, Producer & Creative Director: My expectations are what allows me to be creative. I set the bar and establish my own rules. I try to make myself happy with the work. I am my own biggest critic. When I impress myself, then I figure everyone else will surely be happy too!

———————

Elisa, Speaker, Author & Designer: My biggest obstacle is the incorrect expectation that I should be able to do everything well.

———————

Katrin, CEO: No, I don't think I have had that issue. For me everything is possible. You just need to want it bad enough.

———————

Rob, Program Director & Morning Radio Show Host: Early in my career, I put too much thought into scripting every question for a LIVE interview. I was too focused on my questions and wasn't listening to what the guest was saying. I was already thinking about my next question. I have learned over time that while you have prepared questions, be ready to just listen to the guest and then be ready to go in a new direction depending on their answer.

———————————

Boswick, Circus Performer & Clown: Gawd yes. If I could put a little muzzle on that inner critic I would. The funny thing about that little annoying voice, when I begin any creative process, that critic gets very loud. It never goes away and that unfortunately the longer I do this and the older I get the voice only gets worse.

That's probably the simplest definition of a creative person is they don't give up and push through that voice. Once I begin I have no idea why I procrastinated. But I have to push past that mean inner critic every time.

20. Use Logic

IF CREATIVE THOUGHTS ARE not flowing on their own, try to be logically creative.

By logically creative, I mean create a logical structure around being creative. Define how you will approach the creative process. Perhaps you need a set of rules to structure your day and get yourself into a creative pattern. This will eventually become second nature.

- First, I will clear my work space, or turn on music, or make a cup of coffee.
- On Monday, I will address this or Tuesday, I will do that.

Some people, even creative ones, need structure to their days. Following patterns and rules can help them connect the dots and unlock their creativity. If you're blocked, try making a structured schedule for your creative time.

21. Don't Try to Leave the Earth in a Helium Balloon

—— *ell* ——

EVEN IF YOU HAVE a great idea or solution, improper planning can still cause you to fail.

Building too high without establishing the foundation, skipping steps or moving ahead too fast without using the proper tools could all end with the failure of your idea.

Some vehicles you choose are not the right ones for the job: you cannot leave the earth in a helium balloon, no matter how hard you wish you could.

Take the time to lay out the steps and tools needed for the solution you are forming. Don't just build your castle in the clouds: work on its foundation first.

Creative ideas and projects take planning. No matter how fast you want to proceed, it will still take one step at a time.

22. THINK LIKE AN ADVENTURE TRAVELER

YOU CAN'T HIT THE trail without the gear you need to survive and succeed. Whether it's water purification tablets, bear spray, or good hiking boots, you need certain tools to make sure you have the best chance of success. What are the tools you need for your project or whatever it is that you are creating? Are your tools close at hand?

You *need* to have a creativity toolkit that you can draw from. Your toolkit can be filled with anything, depending on what you're doing. (You can add this book to your kit!)

Here are a few examples of my tools for creating and designing. These are readily available when I want to create:

- pencils, pen and markers of various colors
- scissors, utility knife and Exacto knife
- paper of various sizes, including poster paper
- a journal
- various tapes: clear, duct, paper, electrical, gaffers
- tools: hammer, screwdriver, wrenches, pliers, rechargeable rotary tool etc...

"Reality can be beaten with enough imagination."

-Mark Twain

23. Go for a Walk, Move, Stretch

Stepping away from the project may help overcome the creative block issue. Taking breaks is important. Take the time to move your body and go for a walk, stretch and get your blood flowing, especially if you have been sitting in a chair all day.

Don't be afraid to move around. You can do stretches anywhere you have room, whether in your room or your office or outside. Don't get stuck creatively by sitting still for too long.

Here are some quick exercises & stretches:

- Rotate your neck: up/down, left/right and in circles clockwise/counter clockwise.
- Jumping jacks: even ten will get your blood flowing.
- Arm stretches: loosen your limbs, shake them out, reach for the sky and extend one arm at a time.
- Shift from side to side, foot to foot, slightly bending your knees.

I also highly recommend yoga as a way to cleanse your mind and get some great stretches in for your body and soul.

24. Dim the Lights

DIMMING THE LIGHTS CAN help to set the mood. In a lot of office settings, the lighting is too bright and can lead to headaches or eye fatigue.

If you can't dim the lights in your office or cubicle, find someplace where you can. This also goes for your home. Find a room where you can adjust the lighting and see if that has any effect on your thought process.

You may even find that sitting in the dark is a way to clear your head and allow your creativity to flow without having visual distractions.

If you cannot sit in the dark, close your eyes or get an eye covering that blocks out your surroundings.

Just don't fall asleep if you turn the lights completely out.

25. MEDITATE

MEDITATION IS A RELAXATION technique to calm your mind. Meditation doesn't have to just be sitting cross-legged on the ground with incense burning, candles and saying Ommmmmmm.

You can meditate almost anytime and anywhere. It is a way to self-center and find some inner balance and inner peace. More importantly, meditation can bring the inner calm we sometimes need to clear all the exterior noise.

Meditation is about mindfulness.

Whatever thoughts you may have that come to you while you focus on yourself and your breathing are valid. This is a part of the meditative process.

With repetition and time given to meditation, you'll find that you are able to clear your mind of the surrounding clutter.

Here is a simple exercise that you can do almost anywhere to start exploring meditation:

- Find a comfortable place to sit: either in a chair, on a couch, or on the floor.
- Set a timer for five minutes.
- Close your eyes and focus on yourself.
- Breathe: For the first breath, take a deep breath in through your nose and exhale through your mouth. Now focus on your breath and being calm.
- Try not to focus on any thoughts in particular and try to clear your mind.

Did you find that you were able to clear your mind in the process? Were you finding yourself thinking of work? Did your mind wander to far-off places or perhaps things you have to do later? That's all part of the process.

There is no right or wrong way to meditate. It is a personal experience and a way to cut out some of the clutter and chatter happening around us all the time and maybe find a little bit more of your center.

Q & A With Creatives

ele

Q: How have you broken through creative blocks when you've had them?

Alan, Innovator & Entrepreneur: Go exploring something I know nothing about.

———————

Nick, Producer & Creative Director: I give myself time and patience. The more you force the worse it can be. Take a break, read a book, watch a movie, have a drink, take a walk... I'll try any number of combinations to get my mind off of the problem to allow my subconscious to do a bit of the heavy lifting. Don't be afraid to trust yourself to solve your own problems. Take a nap! It may come to you in a dream.

———————

Elisa, Speaker, Author & Designer: I need to move and hear myself talk it out. Too often, creative blocks are the result of too much disembodied thinking.

———————

Rob, Program Director & Morning Radio Show Host: I would say if you have the luxury of time or are not operating on a tight deadline, the best thing is to walk away. If you are stuck, go for a walk, get something to eat, ride a bike, anything that will take you away from the current project. I have done this with long term projects and have found a fresh perspective always helps.

Barry, Chief Architect/Co-Founder: I stop. I move on to something else, or go for a walk. I talk with a friend — sometimes about the issue, or sometimes completely avoiding the issue. I may stop thinking about the issue for days because I'm frustrated.

Then at some point, it clicks and I try again and I have success. It always feels like when you hit that wall nothing will ever work. Leaving it and coming back seems to work best for me.

Katrin, CEO: I think letting go of the feeling of "must-do-today." I go on a walk, do gardening, photograph flowers, or just be with my kids and husband. Creativity can't be forced. The end result will be mostly frustration.

Boswick, Circus Performer & Clown: I don't believe in creative blocks they strike me as self-indulgent. Creativity is a job and if I treat it that way I can't indulge in the blocks. I wouldn't not go to work because I didn't feel like it. Each creative project is my job. If I'm going to work that day, I have to figure out how to start. So I start. To steal from Nike - "Just do it"

26. DAYDREAM

DAYDREAMING IS A HIGHLY effective technique for generating new ideas. Scientists are discovering that daydreaming is a sign of intelligence and also helps fuel your creative mind.

Let your mind wander. Sometimes drifting thoughts may lead to solving your problem. Perhaps that daydream will clear your head from something else that is blocking you. Allow yourself to have those random bouncing thoughts so you can eventually find your focus.

Start by choosing a place where other people won't bother you. Take a moment to sit back and just let your mind drift.

What would you prefer to be doing right now if you could? Where would you like to travel? Put yourself in the shoes of someone else. What are THEY thinking?

There is more to daydreaming than just wishing you were some place or someone else for a few minutes. As you daydream, you may find that you discover a new concept. Go to your journal and write it down when this occurs.

27. TURN OFF THE PHONE, COMPUTER, AND TV

———— *ele* ————

BE AWARE OF THE devices that may be inadvertently distracting you. You may think they help you be more productive while playing on the side or as background noise. The reality is that they may be hindering you and blocking the creative flow.

We live in a world that is hyper-connected and unfortunately, that connectivity is not always beneficial to fostering creativity and can be a HUGE source of your distractions and failures.

Take a moment before you dive in to your project or creative exercises and physically turn OFF your TV, turn OFF your phone. Give the technology a break and see what happens when you are 100% left with your own thoughts and no other background noises or distractions.

"Imagination is everything.

It is the preview of life's coming attractions."

-Albert Einstein

Q & A WITH CREATIVES

—— *ele* ——

Q: Is THERE ANYTHING you do to get into a creative mindset?

Barry, Chief Architect/Co-Founder: I feel silly saying this, but I pace and talk out loud to myself to get there. I also write all over a white board to try and map out what I need to do. The action of hearing myself and seeing myself describe the problem helps me understand it better. And yes, I have 'arguments' with myself. Especially when trying to wrap my head around a complex situation.

––––––––––

Alan, Innovator & Entrepreneur: A creative mindset has to be something that happens organically for me, it's not a switch. I usually have to work at trying not to chase too many creative thoughts. Creativity stems from stimulation and imagination. There is no "getting into" a creative mindset for me. If I'm trying too hard at something it's usually because I'm up against a deadline and working to fulfill a commitment. I've learned that those two things can be very constrictive and toxic to creative flow.

―――――――

Nick, Producer & Creative Director: I like to take walks in the morning and work/create while I am fresh. I am also inspired by water, most of my best ideas come in the shower! I work in the morning when the gas tank of creativity is at full, and I always work on creative before business (especially budgets!). Throughout the day emails, questions, decisions, errands, all of that noise starts to drain the creative tank. So work fresh, then take breaks and fill the tank!

―――――――

Rob, Program Director & Morning Radio Show Host: I usually focus on what I am trying to achieve. I try to think about how I can make an interview be more interesting to the listener. I think it is important to inject humor whenever possible or appropriate. It makes the guest more relaxed and can give a laugh to the listener. Plus, with LIVE radio, there are no rehearsals and it's that spontaneous factor that helps keep me engaged and creative.

―――――――

Elisa, Speaker, Author & Designer: No matter how intimately personal the creative project, it is only worth anything to anyone else if we are outward-directed. Whether it means just taking a walk or jumping on an airplane to explore somewhere new, I have to get out of my head, into the world, and paying attention.

―――――――

Boswick, Circus Performer & Clown: I shut off distractions. I stop tv, podcasts, avoid the computer and let my mind wander. I have so many projects going at one time that I often get lost in my phone or internet and get nothing done. I put the phone upside down, write down a goal for my project, and just start.

Katrin, CEO: I need a good two hours to get into my creative zone. With everything going on every day, it takes me a long time to disconnect and go into a creative mode. Once in creative mode, I can go on forever. If I'm stuck, I don't push it. I then go gardening or go on a walk with my dogs.

28. Flip a Coin

An arbitrary way to try and force a solution can be as easy as flipping a coin.

Write out a series of questions you need answers to that you are having trouble solving. Make them yes or no questions. These questions are your starting point for brainstorming and can be used whether it's an idea, an issue you're solving, or a new product.

Flip a coin for each question on your list. It's a yes if it comes up heads; tails, is a no. It's highly likely that this procedure will not produce the best outcomes. However, anything is possible.

Have you ever flipped a coin to make a decision, but you already knew you wanted a certain result? Such as flipping a coin for lunch, heads for Chinese and tails for Mexican. Tails comes up and you think, "Gah, I really wanted Chinese food"

Regardless of how you look at it, letting chance decide will force you to rethink your approach to the problem and come up with new solutions.

29. Listen to Music

LISTENING TO MUSIC WHILE you work might help you be more productive or it might distract you. But it's worth a try to see if it stimulates your creativity.

I don't always like to listen to music and whether I do or not depends on the creative project I am working on. If I am building puppets or practicing juggling, I like music. If I am brainstorming, reading or focusing on something new, it's distracting. Music can be inspiring though and I encourage you to find what works for you.

You can create a station in a music streaming app such as Pandora, Spotify, or Apple Music, based on an artist or song that you like. Or create a playlist or station, or use the app's suggestions to find music that will help you focus.

There are even apps specifically designed to provide background music to help you focus. For example, Brain.fm describes itself as "creating functional music" with music that will stimulate your brain into a state of "sustained attention."

30. PLAY AN INSTRUMENT

SOME PEOPLE MIGHT ARGUE that playing an instrument is not inherently creative and that playing someone else's songs, whether by reading sheet music or memory, is simple repetition. I don't believe this.

Playing an instrument can help to get your creativity flowing. How you play is yours and being able to escape from your creative blocks into music may relax you into opening your mind.

Whether you play an instrument well or badly isn't the point: sitting at the piano or strumming the strings of a guitar can help clear your thoughts.

Writing your own music, even if it's just a simple tune, can be like doodling. It's a way to free and open up your mind.

Playing music with friends can also be creatively stimulating. It's not only musicians who can profit from a few hours of jamming together: everyone can.

If you've never played a note of music before, don't be afraid to start. Explore and see where your musical journey takes you.

If you have played an instrument before, experiment with new instruments. If you're a guitarist, drums might be fun. If you play the flute, give a guitar a strum. Try to push yourself.

A willingness to experiment with sounds and an attempt to express yourself is the only requirement of this exercise.

If you don't have access to an instrument, you can use programs and apps to create music on your computer or phone.

Go ahead, make some noise!

31. Use the Magic of "What if?"

─────ele─────

ASKING QUESTIONS CAN BE the answer to creative block. Often, we are not asking enough questions or the right questions to get our answer. The basics of getting information and problem solving comes down to the **5 W's:**

- **Who** is this project it about?
- **What** am I trying to achieve/what happened?
- **When** does it have to happen?
- **Where** will it happen?
- **Why** should it happen?

And #6 -

- **How will it happen?**

Asking these questions as they pertain to your goal is helpful and quite often overlooked.

These six questions may not be relevant to every situation, but at least half can be implemented with almost any topic or project. Ask the 5 W's and you will find yourself closer to answering, **"How will it happen?"**

Q & A With Creatives

Q: **WHAT DREW YOU to this line of work rather than one that could provide better job security and safety?**

Alan, Innovator & Entrepreneur: Today, I do what I do because I wanted better job security years ago. I believe in my abilities and talents far more than any other company ever will, so I bet on myself every day. I'm happy as a self-employed person. As for safety, I learned some valuable lessons during my rock climbing years: understand your strengths and weaknesses, take risks, check your work.

Katrin, CEO: Every day, I leave my desk and my studio looking forward to the next. I wake up with a smile, go to work with a smile, and end my day with a smile. That alone should extend my life by ten years. The fact that I can stay flexible and make decisions based on what clients need gives me the possibility to take care of their pain and struggles. I get the chance to help them overcome fears while going for a win, even if it is just a small one that day. That all just makes me incredibly happy.

———————

Nick, Producer & Creative Director: I have always been driven by passion rather than monetary wealth. I believed, and still do, that while the path might be longer (and harder) it is possible to carve out a happy and meaningful existence making money while still doing the thing that you love.

———————

Barry, Chief Architect/Co-Founder: My line of work (computers and technology) is practical and provides pretty good job security. However, I am taking a risk going the entrepreneurial route. The opportunity is worth the risk and I get to practice being creative often. I have to make ideas work, and come up with solutions to problems on a daily basis.

———————

Boswick, Circus Performer & Clown: I loved seeing plays as a kid, loved Abbott and Costello, old movies and old cartoons and as I grew up, that was my fascination. I remember becoming obsessed with Comedia Del Arte when in High school. Comedia is a style of comic performing from Europe in the 1600s. I even went to see a troupe that performed in that style when I was 17... what a nerd! I've explored other avenues, teaching, working administration in theatre, but I am unable to stay with anything but clowning.

———————

Elisa, Speaker, Author & Designer: I was always an arts kid who loves to daydream. As an entrepreneur, I found a way to see my imaginings become reality and get paid for it.

———————

Rob, Program Director & Morning Radio Show Host: I was drawn to radio because it gives me the opportunity to be creative. You never know exactly what will happen with live radio. Plus, it brings me joy. I love getting up and going to work every day. Did I mention I have to be at work at 4:30 in the morning? I MUST love it.

32. MULTIPLY THE POWER OF WHY?

—ell—

WHEN A PROBLEM ARISES, and you are wondering why, sometimes the best solution is to ask the question of "Why?" multiple times and see where it leads. You may be surprised when the answer comes to you.

Have you ever talked to a small child who asks you "Why?" repeatedly, taking you down a journey of exploration? This is exactly the same concept. It may have seemed annoying at the time, but there is some magic behind it as well.

Asking the question of "Why?" leads to understanding. Sometimes we find ourselves getting into a habit and with no real reason of why we do it that way. Asking the "Why?" can lead to correcting or changing something that wasn't necessarily right but you did not see it until you said it out loud.

The creator of Toyota cars created the five why's method nearly 100 years ago in order to address problems being faced and to find the root of problems. He determined that asking "Why?" five times would lead to a clear definition of the problem and also present the solution.

Write your problem out on a piece of paper or white board and then ask "Why?" Based on that answer, ask "Why?" again and each time it will present you closer to the cause and solution to your problem.

In order to come up with creative solutions and also generate ideas, you can also turn this around in a different way and instead of asking "Why?" five times, use the same method to ask "How?"

This is the power of multiplying the question of "Why?" and also "How?"

33. Play a Game

——— *ele* ———

GAMES ARE HELPFUL TOOLS in creativity and not just a fun way to pass the time with your friends. Playing games can get you out of a rigid mind set, help you step away from your project for a bit, work out strategy and so much more.

You can play games on your own, such as a Rubik's cube, crosswords, solitaire, word jumbles and more. There are also always new mindful and creative games coming out online with one of the newest being Wordle.

Good games for strategy and creative solutions for multiple people include chess, Azul, Pictionary and Scattergories, to name a few. If you don't have anyone to play with, you can also play many of these games online against a computer or random opponents.

There are lots of different games to overcome blocks creatively and also help you to view the world in different way.

One fun example of a creative game for overcoming blocks are creativity dice. There are lots of versions of these. Find the ones that you think best fit you, get a variety of different ones for different tasks or even construct your own that fit your needs.

The idea is a set of die that have different questions or story ideas or scenarios. After rolling you will have a number of key words presented and you then need to connect the dots of the story or path and come up with a solution.

Games of all kinds can stimulate a sense of flow and boost your creativity.

Take a chance, roll the die and go out and play!

"If you want creative workers,

give them enough time to play."

-John Cleese

34. Complete the Drawing

COMPLETING THE DRAWING IS a fun way to think creatively. Draw a random shape such as a V or a swirl or something else and then "complete it."

You can do this exercise solo or with someone else.

Maybe the V becomes the top of a head or the open mouth of a bird or a swirl becomes part of a cloud in the sky. Taking something and turning it into something else can be a good creative exercise for your brain.

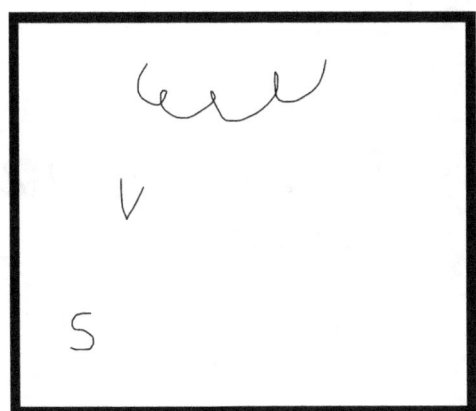

35. Tell Six Word Stories

Six-word stories are an excellent creative challenge. (Feel free to set your own parameters of ten words, three words, etc.) Let your imagination go wild and see what you can come up with with a set, small word count.

One of the more famous six word stories is attributed to Ernest Hemingway: "For sale, baby shoes, never worn."

The same idea may be applied to other forms of media as well. To get your creative juices flowing, you may write a brief song or poetry. You don't need more than six words to produce an effective slogan, tag line or advertisement.

Your creativity just unlocked the magic.

↑

See what I just did there?

36. CREATE A GROUP STORY

You will need to do this exercise in a group setting. It will be more fun with a larger group.

- One person begins by writing down a single word (or a sentence) on a sheet of paper. They hand the paper to a second person.
- The second person writes their own word (or sentence) on the next line, then folds the paper so that the first line is hidden. They hand the paper to a third person.
- The third person can see only the word (or sentence) written by the second person. They write a word of their own, then fold the paper so that the second person's word is hidden and hand the paper on.
- Each person gets a chance to write a word or sentence, but can always only see what's written by the person before.

Depending on the number of people playing, you can go around your circle once or several times. By the time you're done, your story will be strange and completely random. If you compose a tale word by word in this manner, the result will be grammatically incorrect and bizarre.

Q & A With Creatives

———— _eℓℓ_ ————

Q: Does your creative process begin with a clear goal of what you want to achieve in the end?

Alan, Innovator & Entrepreneur: Yes, unless I'm playing just to play. It's fun to go sailing for recreation and just wander around out on the water but a captain with a destination would never set sail without first setting a course.

———————

Nick, Producer & Creative Director: To an extent. You also can't force direction. Be willing to go where ideas flow. When I first conceived of *The Speakeasy*, it was a one-night only gala fundraiser for my non-profit theatre company. Over years of dreaming and imagining it turned into a monstrous 1600 page script with 35 actors and 29 storylines! I never would have guessed in 2006 what I would have finally created almost ten years later!

———————

Rob, Program Director & Morning Radio Show Host: For the most part, yes. I always ask myself and my team members, "What are we trying to accomplish here?" I try to think of how it will either help the company, entertain the listener or preferably both. It is important to not waste the time of yourself or others.

Elisa, Speaker, Author & Designer: Not necessarily. I usually start with an inspiration, a problem to be solved, then I explore ideas and collect random information until something starts to gel.

Barry, Chief Architect/Co-Founder: Yes. I have an idea that I want to implement, or a problem I need to solve. I have to know how something is going to work. I can't leave the process in a "then magic happens" state.

Boswick, Circus Performer & Clown: Having an end goal is very important to me. Something vague like "I'm writing a book" doesn't grab me. But "I'm writing a children's book introducing children to the circus... I can draw from my own life and friends from the circus...This will let me perform more literacy shows for children including schools and libraries."

That example gave me a goal. How can I perform more, how can I make more money? So in writing a book my goal is to bring my show to more kids and families. That's not to say the book itself is not important, but the goal drives the book and quality of the book. If the book is crud, I won't get booked.

37. Think About Worst Case Scenarios

ele

POSITIVE AND FORWARD THINKING comes in handy while coming up with solutions to problems or brainstorming new ideas. You're thinking about what you want to do or what you want to make happen. But in some situations, thinking backwards and thinking of the worst case scenario is extremely useful.

Think about all of the possibilities and especially about what you _don't_ want to happen instead of what you do want to happen.

You may, for example, set out to create something that solves a specific issue that your target audience is experiencing. Take a step back and consider, "Could your clients be harmed by your product?" Think about it this way, and maybe you'll have a better sense of what the product **has** to have.

Focus on the things you'd rather not convey. Is there anything you don't want someone to associate with your work?

The more you can focus on what you don't want to do or don't want your project to be, the clearer your solution will become.

"Never wait for tomorrow, what if tomorrow never comes?"

-Elvis Presley

38. Practice Creative Clouding

CREATIVE CLOUDING IS A term I coined almost 20 years ago. The concept is simple and you likely already know it and have maybe even done it yourself. But ever since I was a kid, I've looked for images in the clouds and have been fascinated with clouds of all shapes and sizes.

So, look at the clouds and see what images you can find in them. They are forever changing shapes and have stories to be told. You can find people or animals or fantasy characters such as dragons, and so much more.

Then take this one step further, and ask yourself, "Why"?

"Why is that dragon in the sky"?

"What is the turtle doing? Where is he going?"

You can come up with some fun and elaborate stories and see where it takes you.

The next time you are outside, I highly recommend you look toward the sky.

39. Reward Yourself

~~~~~~~~

REWARDING YOURSELF FOR A goal is a good thing to do and can lead to positive reinforcement. This doesn't have to be anything elaborate or if it's a big goal with a big payoff for you in the end, then by all means make it a big reward.

If you are stuck working on an idea, you can set a goal of, "If I do this, I can have a coffee break or watch a movie."

If you are accomplishing a big goal or project and can overcome it, perhaps you say, "I will buy myself a new gadget," or something similar.

Sometimes having a goal in mind and having a physical reward at the end will give you the push you need to finish.

At the end of my first big cruise ship contract, I bought myself a watch that I wear on special occasions. It always reminds me of that accomplishment.

40. Write 100 Questions

―――ℓℓℓℓ―――

THIS CAN BE A fun exercise and also more challenging than you might expect. I first heard about this idea about 20 years ago in Michael Gelbs' book, *How to Think Like Leonardo da Vinci: Seven Steps to Genius Every Day.*

The exercise is simple: Write 100 questions. These questions can be about anything. Write questions about your idea or questions about a problem you are trying to solve.

You do not need to have the answers to these questions. You will find the first ten or so questions come super easily. As the 100 questions go on, it gets increasingly difficult and often times a struggle for the last ten to twenty.

The exercise is not only about the questions but also about discovering an emerging pattern. Look through your questions and see if any are the same question but worded differently. Look for groupings of similar topics or ideas.

Circle those questions that repeat and focus on those as there is some sort of answer for you to be discovered there.

"Everything you can imagine is real."

-Pablo Picasso

41. Combine Multiple Ideas

ele

YOU WILL HAVE LOTS of ideas and feel some of them may even be brilliant at times.

But what if nothing is sticking and you aren't getting the idea where you want it to be?

Or perhaps the idea works, but you don't know quite where to put it in the grand scheme of your vision.

Perhaps the key is to join ideas together and connect the dots that way. This technique works great when creating a routine for a show.

Years ago, I was working on different ways to spin balls, rather than just on my finger or a stick. I started to spin balls on a variety of things, from nails to rubber chickens to ice cream cones. Eventually, I used all of these ideas in different shows, years apart.

The idea of cones for the ball spin eventually lead to me creating an ice cream show for Cold Stone Creamery and a variety of ice cream related routines followed. Years later, the technique became part of my ice cream show, which I perform at fairs and festivals.

The idea of using rubber chickens for the ball spin became a prominent part of my Rubber Chicken Show and I used the nails for a corporate event for a construction company.

Combining ideas can lead to presenting your ideas in new ways and provide you with new opportunities.

42. Visualize

HAVE YOU EVER HEARD the saying, to dream it is to be it? You may likely know what you want for the end goal of your project.

Take a few moments and physically write out what you want with full details. This helps make it real and tangible if it is merely an idea.

Make a one week plan, a one month plan, or even a five year plan. Imagine you already have the things you want to achieve and now just need to work the steps to get there.

Create smaller, more easily digestible goals for each of those steps. Map out each step needed to get to and from the next and stick with your plan you just created.

Or work from the end goal and move backwards step by step.

Sometimes starting at the end can help you to overcome blocks you are facing at the beginning or in the middle. It helps to define the problem that you are trying to overcome and to have your end goal in mind.

Q & A With Creatives

_____ *ele* _____

Q: How do you go from an idea in your head to a completed creative action?

Alan, Innovator & Entrepreneur: Work it backwards. I focus on the end result and work every step backwards to the very beginning. I have to, in a very detailed sense, imagine what it is I'm trying to create and why I am trying to create it before I can ever imagine how to create it.

Nick, Producer & Creative Director: Deadlines. Creativity is nothing without a goal. Anyone can have an idea, ideas are cheap. Execution is the hard part. I manage my time and expectations, and then I am not too hard on myself when I fall short. You can't force creativity and sometimes you just aren't feeling it. Instead of beating yourself up, you breathe and come back to it fresh. Also, sometimes you just have to force yourself to write. Trust that even your garbage will be somewhat good and then let tomorrow self clean it up.

Rob, Program Director & Morning Radio Show Host: I prefer to sketch or write it out if possible. With LIVE radio, I might not get the chance to plan too far in advance. However, if it is longer term project, such as planning a radio contest, creating a new talk show or planning a remote broadcast, I like to write out my ideas and read them aloud.

———————

Barry, Chief Architect/Co-Founder: I begin with pacing and talking about the idea. I verbalize and internalize what it is that needs to happen. If I'm near my white board, I write down key parts of the idea, and then some steps I can take to make the idea work. Then, more pacing, and more writing.

Once I lay out a few steps that lead in the direction I need to go, I begin researching software and technologies that appear to do what I need them to do. This often leads to more pacing, more talking, and more writing. Then, at some point, it 'clicks' and the idea falls into place. I seem to finally understand what I need to do and how to go about doing it. Now, I can draft up the plan for real. This entire process can take a couple of hours, or days or weeks depending on the challenge.

———————

Elisa, Speaker, Author & Designer: Big ideas are just that – big. They need to be taken in smaller chunks with each piece given meticulous attention. Only then can the pieces be assembled. Bottom line, I keep a pretty detailed to-do list.

———————

Boswick, Circus Performer & Clown: Everything has a deadline so I try to work backwards. Even if it's artificial and arbitrary. If the creative idea is vague you still want it done by a certain point. I imagine what it looks like and what has to happen step-by-step.

———————

Katrin, CEO: My new ideas mostly come to me during the night or early morning hours when I'm half awake and half asleep. But first, I have my morning coffee. After that, I jot everything down that came to me during the night. I create a mind map on a big paper and let my thoughts come out, unedited. For my new ideas that have possibilities to grow, I involve my husband, as he knows the business well.

I do a ton of research but very quickly. I don't get hung up on minor details. Then I create a project plan. I use a board and post-it notes. Write down the main action steps I need to take, and below the main steps, I display the mini steps for each action point.

Often I build a beta version or create a beta product and run it by a group of aromatherapists. I do a soft launch first, take in the reaction and feedback, make it better, and launch the final product.

43. Create a Vision Board

DURING YOUR CHILDHOOD, DID you ever make magazine collages or vision boards? It's never too late to get out the scissors and go to work on creating a vision board.

Making a vision board is a fun way to get your creative juices flowing. It helps you visualize your end goal and can inspire you.

Take a piece of poster board and grab a few magazines. Go through them to find words or images that you can use. Every time you see an image that represents your goal, you can tape or glue it to the board to create a vision of what you want. This is a great way of reusing old magazines or papers you may have laying around.

Either select a theme or cut at random and see how it comes together. It's up to you whether you want to set a future goal, tell a tale, or make an argument for your idea with your collage. When you combine a variety of images, words and materials, you may develop new ideas that could lead to other forms of creative work or something to strive toward.

44. Use Mind Mapping

—ece—

MIND MAPPING IS A great way to visualize a thought process. Mind mapping is a simple, visual, useful tool to connect the dots of your thought process, to develop an associations list, to brainstorm and to organize all the relative information around an idea.

Think of a mind map as being like a tree. You start with the root idea or word and then create off-shoots and branches. You explore the associations from that core root word. Within those off-shoots you can have subcategories or little fruits that help to refine your ideas. You can see an example on the next page.

The human brain can handle somewhere around a maximum of 8 - 10 initial offshoots of a root idea. You don't need more than that. Five to six initial association offshoots from your original idea is fine.

A good free online tool for mind mapping can be found through MindMup: https://app.mindmup.com/

I use mind mapping when working out new routines and ideas. I start with my lead topic and then create an association list around it. With this association list in hand, I can then look for connectors and work on the next phase of my scripting or routine. Let's look at a mind map outline and how it works.

As an example, we can use a fire routine I was working on. My lead topic will be: Fire

Some of my free associations and ideas are fire-related:

hot, flame, burn, blaze fuel, torch, glow, spark

(These are just a few. There are many more possibilities.)

You can also add pictures or other ideas that may connect, or you can offshoot from fire again and instead of flame, maybe reference another type of fire:

gun, launch, blast, discharge, firing

I could have a smaller offshoot of any of the words that have multiple meanings, like:

Hot = heat, attractive, etc...

Blast = explosion, having fun, etc...

I try to think of all the things I can to connect the initial topic and then narrow down all the information into one place to see it more clear.

After I have my mind map and associations, I look for words with double meanings. Perhaps I could find a joke to add to my routine about "Hot," not in reference to heat, but meaning attractive, or perhaps I could connect the word "Blast," not referring to an explosion, but meaning "having fun with it." What a blast!

Here is an example of mind mapping from the center ideas showing how thoughts branch out into sub thoughts and categories:

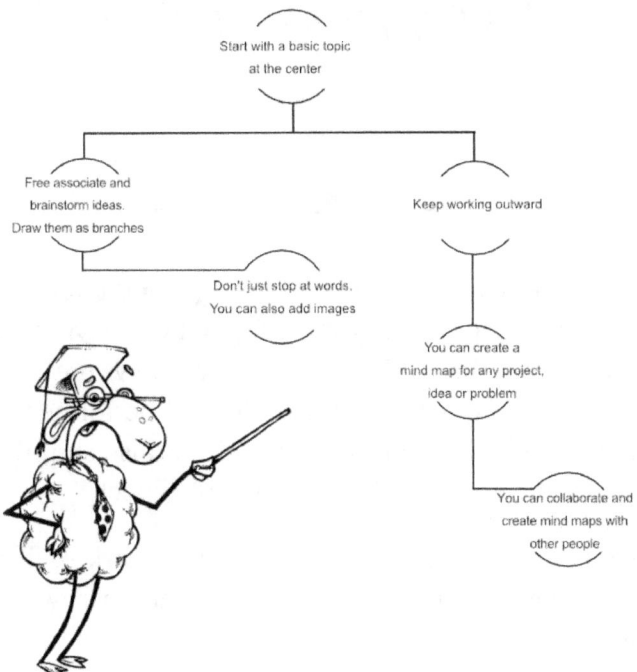

45. Be Who You Are & Do What You Do

BEFORE PERFORMING ON A cruise ship stage for the very first time, I found myself experiencing stage-fright. I was having a panicked moment. Even though I had done many shows previously, spoken in front of thousands of people, and performed on stages and at festivals around the world, the cruise ship was a new venue for me and I didn't know what to expect.

What if the ship is rocking? Will my sound work? Will my tricks work on unstable surfaces? These and other fears were preying on my mind.

I phoned a performer friend of mine and he gave me the advice I needed to hear:

"Just go out there and do what you do."

I can not tell you how many times I have found myself worried about my tools or parts of my performance before walking out on a stage or working on another project. When I pause to breathe, I repeat those words to myself. It almost always brings a sense of calm.

Be yourself. Be who you are and let others appreciate what you bring to the table. You are unique and awesome, and you know what? It's okay to be creative and create and do what you want. Go ahead, be different. Feel confident to have weird ideas. Don't suppress them. Say them out loud, and let them become part of the process.

If you aren't being yourself, people will see through your deception. It's like using an alias for who you really are, and in the end, it will always be found out.

Be you and think like you think and allow your mindset to be your own.

Be who you are and do what you do!

"Don't be afraid of being different. Be afraid of being the same as everyone else"

-Anonymous

Q & A With Creatives

ell

Q: WHEN FACED WITH a hurdle or creative block, what's a piece of advice have you been given that has stayed with you?

Alan, Innovator & Entrepreneur: It's not about you. Get over yourself.

———————

Katrin, CEO: Don't give up. If it is not here today, it will come back tomorrow. Just make sure you are not giving up.

———————

Barry, Chief Architect/Co-Founder: A great math teacher in high school always said "If you don't know what to do, do what you know". I took that to mean that you have to start somewhere. Get something going. Then, as you're in it, it keeps developing. It has always stuck with me.

———————

Boswick, Circus Performer & Clown: I often go back to what my friend, magician Jay Alexandar, once told me, he said "doing something is always better than doing nothing." People get so stopped they end up doing nothing. Everyone wants a perfect project, that's human. Picasso at one point had to buy a brush, paints and put something on canvas. Even if he hated it he started.

Elisa, Speaker, Author & Designer: I worked with an acting coach for many years who said people can always spot what's fake. A creative block means we are trying to push through what does not come naturally, what isn't real. When I can get back in touch with what is authentically true for me, the blocks fall down.

Rob, Program Director & Morning Radio Show Host: When faced with a hurdle, I've discovered a useful way to find a solution is to turn to my team. It's very helpful to bounce ideas off my coworkers. Someone once told me that when you need to create, sometimes it's best to collaborate. You have to learn to trust your team and find the best solution.

Q: What suggestions do you have for those who want to improve their creative abilities?

Alan, Innovator & Entrepreneur: Ask a lot of questions to those who you respect and admire the most in your field. Then, seriously shut up and let them answer. Become a student of your craft and surround yourself with the knowledge that will help you most.

———————

Rob, Program Director & Morning Radio Show Host: I think it's important to be relaxed and focused. Do not overthink it. Yes, be clear about what you want achieve, but enjoy the process. Also, be able to think outside the box. In radio, someone told me "Your least favorite song, could be someone's favorite." So, don't think your way is the only way. Be open to the possibilities that there are other ways.

———————

Katrin, CEO: Join like-minded groups and accountability pods and find a good partner or friend who supports you. Another would be to always just start. Don't stay in your head, creating sabotaging thoughts. Share your thoughts with others, take in reactions, and then use the helpful comments and let go of the rest.

———————

Nick, Producer & Creative Director: Creativity is a muscle. You want to get strong? Use it or lose it. The more you condition yourself the easier and faster the ideas will flow.

———————

Elisa, Speaker, Author & Designer: Practice letting go of judgment. The constant stream of judgment that runs through most of our minds stops us from being creative before we ever even try.

———————

Barry, Chief Architect/Co-Founder: I don't have much of an answer here that doesn't sound like a fluffy "just keep at it" kind of answer. I don't think what I do is all that creative. I'm just solving problems I need to solve, or coming up with ideas that address needs I have observed. One thing I have picked up along the way in my area of work is to learn all about a software or technology well enough to be able to come up with creative uses for it that may not be the exact use for which it was intended.

———————

Boswick, Circus Performer & Clown: Find something that requires using your mind and your body at one time. Cooking, baking, gardening, cleaning. I like buying a flower and repotting it. Something about dirt, plants and using your hands then cleaning the mess up makes me feel very creative. Find something like that in your life. I think these physical activities of something you are good at and enjoy, put you in a creative space. These examples are small projects, repotting a plant or making bread take 30 minutes and they have a nice ending. You'll find your mind is quiet and you can create more easily.

46. STOP THINKING ABOUT IT

—— *ele* ——

SOMETIMES IT HELPS TO stop thinking about the problem in order to solve it. How many times have you struggled to remember some piece of information, then had it pop into your brain as soon as you've given up. Then you think, "How could I have forgotten that?"

Sometimes the solution to a block is to step away from it for a little bit and come back in five minutes, five hours or even tomorrow. Even when facing a deadline, if you aren't getting anywhere, take a break and come back to your project with fresh thoughts and fresh eyes.

It's better to let an idea develop naturally than to push it. Don't try to force an idea when it's just not there. It may be easier to put it off until the next day and deal with the problem in the morning when you're feeling more rested.

Sleep can also be a great source of new ideas. Maybe you'll dream about the issue or your current creative project. Perhaps you'll have a flash of inspiration when you first open your eyes in the morning.

47. FIND YOUR BEST CREATIVITY TIME

WHAT TIME DO YOU feel that you are most productive? We all have a time that we are most alert and creative. I have never worked well under a "normal" work schedule.

For me, I find my mornings are a time to relax, drink my morning coffee, and catch up on the daily news. After lunch, I can get into a creative groove and rhythm, and then work well into the night.

This is not a steadfast rule, of course, and creativity motivation can strike at any moment. In fact, this passage of the book was written in the morning. But as a general guide, I find afternoons/evenings work best creatively for me.

If you are hitting blocks on a regular basis, maybe the answer is to try a different time to work on your problem.

Analyze your daily schedule and find when you are most productive and log that in your journal. If you are most creative in the morning, afternoon or evening, set a reminder for yourself to use that time as part of your structured creative day.

48. Find Your Best Creativity Place

———— *ele* ————

THE OTHER PART OF this equation is *where* are you most productive?

Not only is there a best time for us to be creative and productive, we also all thrive in our own best productive and creative places.

Perhaps your place is an art studio, a library, or your office. Perhaps sitting on the couch with your laptop or cooking in the kitchen is best for you.

It also helps to be aware of whether you are more or less productive based on how many people are around you.

Maybe you thrive best with lots of people around or in front of a large audience, or maybe you are more introverted and work best with absolute silence and no interruptions.

Be consciously aware of where you are most productive and feel your creative brain starting to work best and try to implement and recreate that into your regular daily process.

Q & A With Creatives

—eee—

Q: WHY DID YOU decide to pursue the job or artistic route that you have chosen to follow? Did something or someone influence you?

Alan, Innovator & Entrepreneur: It took years before I realized I was an artist. In fact, it wasn't until someone called me an artist that I ever considered I was one. I was following what looked like the most fun and rewarding way to live and still pay my bills. Many people influenced my decisions along the way and I am constantly in awe of the crazy cool talents my friends possess. I didn't know how to sing, or juggle, or walk on stilts, or paint.....or really hardly anything that I thought defined an artist. It took years for me to find my niche. I just kept falling forward.

————————

Nick, Producer & Creative Director: I remember seeing my older siblings perform in church youth group and variety shows. I was a bit younger so didn't get to participate. I think in some way I was fulfilling something that I wasn't allowed to do long,

long ago. Now I am motivated by audiences and helping elicit their reactions, whatever those may be.

———————

Rob, Program Director & Morning Radio Show Host: I grew up listening to radio as a child. I would hear talk radio at whisper level coming out of my parents' bedroom. It was around the age of 12 or 13 that I started to think about radio as a career. I created my own 'fake' radio station to practice and emulate the disc jockeys, newscasters and hosts whom I admired. One of my favorite personalities is Tom Bergeron, who was hosting the morning show on WBZ-AM 1030 in Boston while I was in High School.

———————

Barry, Chief Architect/Co-Founder: I have tended to always gravitate towards computers. I found the machines to be fascinating. I like logic and computers fit that nicely.

Creating this company was a partnership with my colleague that came out of the previous company he started. We were going around educating people in companies how to manage their information using existing technologies from a well-known software company. We slowly recognized that the existing technology was too cumbersome. Even if the people applied what they learned in our training, they probably weren't going to labor through the process to implement it. We saw an opportunity to create a better solution to the existing problem.

———————

Boswick, Circus Performer & Clown: I just loved old comedy as a kid. I watched Abbott and Costello every Sunday before Sunday school. Bugs Bunny, Our Gang, Marx Brothers. I'd say my biggest influences were from television and Mad Magazine. Also I was inspired by the amazing Bill Irwin. He's famous as Mr Noodle on Sesame Street. I've just loved following his career. He was a huge influence on what I could become. I read a profile of him in The New Yorker and said, "That's who I want to be."

———————

Katrin, CEO: The family on my dad's side has always been entrepreneurs. I started selling ice cream at a very young age as my grandma owned an ice-cream shop.

My fascination with Essential Oils has been there since the age of 11. I was more on the alternative side of health solutions and preventive care than covering up symptoms with medicine. I always had my kids pass their fever, cough, and stomachaches without large interference. I felt it was essential to let the body "do its thing." I studied Aromatherapy, created a software for Essential Oil Enthusiasts with my husband (a programmer), and launched a course and membership to help other Aromatherapists become successful.

———————

Elisa, Speaker, Author & Designer: I remember my dad telling me after he got out of the military that he just wanted an opportunity to be his own boss. Not everyone has that opportunity, but it became my goal. I love creating work that would not exist in the world if I didn't create it.

49. Slow It Down

SLOWING DOWN IS A great approach to improve your ability to be more perceptive, which is needed for creativity.

Slow any routine thing you perform on a daily basis down to a crawl.

Slowly prepare to brew your morning cup of coffee, pay attention to every detail of the process you take in making it, from scooping the grinds to how you prepare it to drink.

Pay attention to each and every action you perform and how it makes you feel.

Throughout your day, pay close attention to your views of the world around you. Take in the sights and sounds as you go.

Most people lose out on excellent ideas in their daily lives because we stop paying attention.

Work on honing your sense of observation and you will see changes in how you look at projects you are working on.

50. STEP AWAY FROM IT

~~eee~~

STEPPING AWAY FROM A project for a while can be a great way to re-approach it with fresh eyes and perhaps new ideas. Perhaps stepping away is for just a few minutes, a few hours or days... or maybe it turns into months or even years!

Of course, if you are on a deadline, you may not have months or years or even days. Whatever the time frame for your project, hopefully you can take a breather from it from time to time and step away if you find yourself blocked.

I recently came back around to a project of mine with some ideas that had been in my notebooks for nearly 15 years. When the timing was right, the idea came back around to present itself.

As a child, I always had a love of puppetry. I grew up watching _The Muppet Show_ and how Jim Henson and his team brought those characters to life and I loved that style of puppet work.

In my mid 20s, I learned some puppet building skills and played around with that muppet style foam puppet building. I also joined a found object puppet troupe in San Francisco, dabbling with puppetry here and there and learning to foster the lives of inanimate objects and bring them to "life."

But I never felt able to give puppetry the proper focus needed if I wanted to do more with it. My puppet ideas mostly filled pages of my notebook.

It became something that I used to do. It became ideas that I had for doing "someday". Over the years of my schedule of performing, traveling and family, my puppetry endeavors and those ideas took a back seat.

In the midst of the global pandemic of 2020, I couldn't travel or perform. Other performers were trying their hand at virtual shows, something I did not feel my juggling show would translate well to. I found that the idea of puppetry and puppet building came back to me as the solution. I was able to revive the idea and give it a new go.

Out of that came a whole new project for me, one that I truly enjoyed: *PuppetWork*. Stepping away for years paid off with plenty of ideas and fresh eyes.

51. Start Over

ⲉⲗⲗ

ALMOST NO CREATIVE VENTURE project is done or perfected on the first try. There are refinements and reworks.

Sometimes we hit a block and refuse to see starting over as a potential solution, because we put so much time and work into it, but sometimes starting over **is** the solution.

When writing a book, even this one, there are multiple rough drafts. After a few days or months of stepping away from it or taking it from the creative room into the critique room, it sometimes still became apparent that I maybe had to start over again. Not entirely from scratch, but I had to throw out — or put aside I should say — some parts that didn't quite fit.

Perhaps they will find their way into the *next* book project.

So ask yourself, "What would you do if you were to start over?"

I am not saying to scrap your ideas entirely and throw it away... remember your journals?

Tuck the thought or idea away in your journal and you can go back and revisit it later. Perhaps you'll forget all about it and months or even years later, come back around to the idea and see it with fresh eyes and maybe a fresh solution or with more information to address it.

If you are spending days or weeks or months or longer trying to overcome a block and it's not happening, maybe it's time to start again from scratch.

With any creative project, sometimes you have to be willing and able to cut your losses. Starting again is part of the creative process.

"Don't let the noise of other's opinions drown out your own inner voice"

-Steve Jobs

Q & A WITH CREATIVES

ele

Q: HOW DO YOU tell when an item or project is done and does not need any more work?

Elisa, Speaker, Author & Designer: I don't believe creative work is every fully 'done.' But I know when I'm at the 'good enough' stage when further iterations or improvements start getting really nit-picky.

_____

Nick, Producer & Creative Director: After I have reviewed the work countless times and can't stand to look at it anymore I put it down. Then maybe come back a few days or week or so later. If it still makes me smile and I can hear the authenticity of the work in my head, then I call it. Also, deadlines sometimes dictate when it's done.

_____

Alan, Innovator & Entrepreneur: Everything I do needs more work. I had to learn to eventually be ok with "good enough." However, there is a huge difference between allowing your work to be "good enough" and having an attitude of "good enough" when it comes to your art. One allows you to move on, the other is a byproduct of apathy.

––––––––––

Barry, Chief Architect/Co-Founder: It never ends. :)

Much of my work is an evolution based on what the results of an original idea comes out as. It gets built, and then gets tested, and then draws feedback. That feedback often drives changes to the original idea. Bithoop, as an example, has undergone many transformations and it hasn't been released yet. However, the software is still true to its original roots. The methods of going about it have changed.

––––––––––

Boswick, Circus Performer & Clown: When I have to present or turn in the project I do as good a job as I can in the time I'm allowed. Sometimes I'll work on something till I can't stand it anymore. I work on pretty rigid deadlines so I don't have that luxury to tinker forever.

––––––––––

Katrin, CEO: I don't think that exists. Maybe it is just me, but I always find ways to make things better, faster, or just more beautiful. That's why I launch imperfect. It will never be done otherwise.

Q: If you had to start over, would you choose a different path?

Alan, Innovator & Entrepreneur: I start over every day. I have plenty of paths to choose from and I count my blessings that I do. I can't change what was, only focus on what can be.

Nick, Producer & Creative Director: Every single time. Why walk the same path twice? Where's the fun in that?

Rob, Program Director & Morning Radio Show Host: Not at all. As long as I can still talk, I want to be on the radio!

Barry, Chief Architect/Co-Founder: I love what I do. I have found an area that is a good fit for me. There is a high overlap between something I am good at and something I like to do. That overlap keeps me very interested in it and makes innovating and problem solving pretty fun and exciting. I do wish however, I trusted myself when I was much younger [too young to realize] and actually stick to my strengths and pursue education in computers. My undergraduate degree was in film. I feel it would have helped me advance my skills even further now. Live and learn.

Elisa, Speaker, Author & Designer: Never. I would just get on the path sooner.

Katrin, CEO: If I had known what I know now, I would just launch everything sooner and imperfect. I wouldn't be afraid of competition; I would simply fall on my nose sooner and more often, but also get to my goal faster. I was way too scared to put myself out there for a good part of my entrepreneurial career. I wish I could have shaken that off sooner.

———————

Boswick, Circus Performer & Clown: I think the very definition of an artist is you don't have a choice — this is what you have to do despite the financial downsides and risks to your personal relationships. But if I could go back and talk to the young clown I was way back, I'd give advice on how to get where I am now much faster with less mistakes.

So I guess...NO!

"There's a way to do it better – find it."
Thomas A. Edison

AFTERWORD

Creativity and innovation have no boundaries; the ideas presented here are merely the beginning of a journey that will take you far and wide.

Creative thinking is one of the most wonderful and significant things that exists on our planet, in my opinion. Without our initial ideas, conceived by our imagination, we are unable to innovate or overcome unforeseeable obstacles in our path.

Not only are artists, innovators, and entrepreneurs capable of generating new ideas and inventions, but so are all of us. Creativity is present in everyone, and it is always possible to see the world and our goals with new and fresh eyes.

I have provided you now with a collection of tools and techniques on how you can add more ideas to your creativity toolbox and showed you some examples of where it has helped me.

The way we do something does not always have to be the same, especially in today's ever changing world. The fact that you have a voice, thoughts, and innovative ideas is always a great thing!

We are surrounded by creativity and innovative solutions; we live in a creative environment flourishing all around us. Make an effort each and every day to be creative in some manner for yourself; this is your responsibility.

Work to look at situations with fresh eyes and come up with fresh ideas on a regular basis; keep that journal close by and hunt for a new and creative solution whenever you get the chance.

We experience creativity in a variety of ways and from a variety of sources, including not only our own thoughts but also those of our friends, family, teachers and coworkers, among other people. Pay attention to them while you're working on your creativity because they may present their own point of view that will help you further develop your ideas.

Creativity and innovation are not just thoughts, but also a skill and a muscle to be cultivated and exercised.

Explore several creative approaches and don't just quit after one attempt; repetitions are essential to your growth and success, just as in any form of physical activity, such as lifting weights. With practice, some aspects of creativity will become easier, because you are teaching your brain to think in a more creative and solution-oriented manner.

I hope this book sparks your originality and imagination.

Appendix 1

—ℓℓℓ—

THE QUESTIONS ON CREATIVITY that I believe that are best to ask myself, my colleagues and coaching clients are the following:

Questions:

- What do you think it means to be creative?
- What drew you to this line of work rather than one that could provide better job security and safety?
- Why did you decide to pursue the job or artistic route that you have chosen to follow? Did something or someone influence you?
- As a creative person/having a job that requires creative solutions, what was one of the toughest obstacles you had to overcome?
- Do you have any tricks or tips for keeping yourself interested and excited about your projects or work?
- Is there anything you do to get into a creative mindset?
- How do you go from an idea in your head to a completed creative action?
- Does your creative process begin with a clear goal of what you want to achieve in the end?

- How do you tell when an item or project is done and does not need any more work?
- Have you ever felt like your own expectations stopped you from being creative?
- How have you broken through creative blocks when you've had them?
- When faced with a hurdle or creative block, what's a piece of advice have you been given that has stayed with you?
- What suggestions do you have for those who want to improve their creative abilities?
- If you had to start over, would you choose a different path?

I encourage you to ask yourself these questions and write the answers in your journal.

Appendix II

—— *ell* ——

VOICES

Allow me to introduce you to my panel who answered, in their own words, my questions about their paths and creative solutions to overcoming obstacles:

Barry Baronas - Chief Architect/Co-Founder of Bithoop

Barry Baronas researches software and infrastructure technologies, focusing on innovative ways to use them in the development of Bithoop, an intelligent work management solution. He determines how the application should work, what steps and processes need to happen, what data to gather, how to formulate logic using the data he has, and how to deliver results to end users.

Barry doesn't do the programming, but does determine what his development team needs to do to make it all come together.

You can visit the website at: www.BitHoop.com

Katrin Birkholz - CEO of Blend Precisely and Blend Precisely Academy

Blend Precisely is a software business toolkit for Aromatherapists, Herbalists and Cosmetic Formulators. It allows you to create safe and profitable blends, formulations, and products using Essential Oils and Herbs.

Blend Precisely provides safety information and graphical representations of the dilution ratio and blend percentage to alert the user about potential hazardous blends.The goal of Blend Precisely and Blend Precisely Academy is to provide tools and knowledge to support anyone using Essential Oils for business and to help accelerate and inspire new ideas.

You can visit the website at: www.BlendPrecisely.io

Alan Bruess - Innovator & Entrepreneur

Alan Bruess is an innovator, problem solver and creative consultant. Alan has conceived and built a number of unique projects over the years, including a kids' pedal tractor pull that explains drag and weight distribution. He's had exhibits with solar powered cars and taught fair-goers about energy and conservation with a number of kinetic contraptions. He has built large, interactive exhibits for Washington State Fair showcasing the farming industry and also has created and hosted a successful podcast with Tailgate Entertainer showcasing various people within the County and State Fair industry.

Alan has also recently created a successful coffee company with Frog Hopper Coffee.

Rob Hakala - Program Director & Morning Host at 95.9 WATD-FM in Marshfield, MA.

Rob Hakala hosts a five-hour weekday morning news program, hosting and interviewing guests while also keeping things moving so newscasts, traffic, weather and sports all air on time. As Program Director, Rob is responsible for shaping and maintaining the sound of WATD and their sister station WBMS 101.1 FM and AM 1460 in Brockton Massachusetts.

You can visit the website at: www.959WATD.com

Elisa Hays - "Empathy Evangelist" - speaker, author, designer... not necessarily in that order.

Elisa listens to people, tells stories, and creates ways to live more kindly

You can visit the website at: www.ElisaHays.com

David Magidson (Boswick) - Circus Performer & Clown

Boswick is a former clown with Ringling Brothers and Barnum & Bailey Circus. He's appeared in commercials, on TV shows, and in movies, such as *Milk* starring Sean Penn.

Boswick was profiled in New York Magazine and has been entertaining families for more than half his life and appeared at over 5000 events. Boswick's world-famous balloon animals have appeared in publications and on TV shows and now Boswick has his own TV show on Saturday mornings.

You can visit the website at: www.BoswickTheClown.com

Nick A. Olivero - Producer & Creative Director

Nick A. Olivero is a creator and producer of live theatrical immersive experiences. He develops wildly imaginative artistic concepts, writes, directs and curates interactive guest experiences.

He co-founded and is the Executive Director of Boxcar Theatre; notable credits include: *Clue*, *Hedwig and the Angry Inch*, *Little Shop of Horrors*, and *The Speakeasy*. He has been creating and producing theatre for over two decades in San Francisco.

ACKNOWLEDGMENTS

This book was made a reality with lots of support and I want to thank the people who helped make it possible.

I want to thank my son Max for always being there. The love he shows, his kindness and his amazing creativity has no bounds.

Thanks to Christina Pearson for her love; for supporting my crazy ideas; and for helping me feel home here in Florida.

Thank you so much to these friends for all of their help, insights and contributions to this book: Barry Baronas, Katrin Birkholz, Alan Bruess, Rob Hakala, Elisa Hays, David Magidson, Nick A. Olivero and Rachel Peters.

Thanks to these friends for the brainstorming sessions, helping me with edits and the grammar changes: Karen Gibson, Dan Holzman, Scott Meltzer and especially Wendy Sharp on the one. Wendy, I could not have finished this project without you.

About the Author

Greg Frisbee is a speaker and creativity coach who specializes in innovation and thinking beyond the box.

He has been performing all over the world for over 20 years, bringing a distinctive brand of humor along with juggling, magic and variety skills along with him.

In order to cultivate and encourage creativity and creative problem solving, as well as to assist people in overcoming adversity, Greg created *Sheep Theory: Think Outside the Flocks*.

Using ideas from this book, Greg thinks you will find solutions to overcome obstacles you are facing, expand your creativity toolkit, and be more effective creatively in a variety of situations.

Greg also has a degree in Media and Communications, which allows him to turn on and off computers, program televisions, and brew a fantastic cup of coffee.